T H E   S T A R R Y   S K Y

Comets
and
Shooting Stars

P a t r i c k   M o o r e
Illustrated by Paul Doherty

Riverswift

First published 1994

1 3 5 7 9 10 8 6 4 2

Copyright © Aladdin Books Limited 1994
An Aladdin Book
Designed and produced by
Aladdin Books Limited
28 Percy Street
London W1P 9FF

Design: David West Children's Book Design

This edition published in the United Kingdom in 1996 by
Riverswift, Random House, 20 Vauxhall Bridge Road, London SW1V 2SA

Illustrations by Paul Doherty
Additional illustrations by Mike Lacey and Ian Thompson
Photocredits: Pages16 and 72: Science Photo Library; page 28: Melies
(Courtesy Kobal Collection); page 32: Frank Spooner Pictures; pages 36 and
37: Roger Vlitos

Random House Australia (Pty) Limited, 20 Alfred Street, Milsons Point, Sydney,
New South Wales 2061, Australia

Random House New Zealand Limited, 18 Poland Road, Glenfield, Auckland
10, New Zealand

Random House South Africa (Pty) Limited, PO Box 337, Bergvlei, South Africa

Random House UK Limited Reg. No. 954009

A CIP catalogue record of this book is available from the British Library

ISBN 0 099679 01 9

Printed in Hong Kong

*My grateful thanks are due to Paul Doherty for his splendid
pictures, and to Lynn Lockett for all her help and encouragement.*

P.M.

Contents

The sun and the moon as seen from Earth.

The sun and its family

All our light comes from the sun. It is so bright that you must never look straight at it or you will hurt your eyes badly. The sun is much bigger

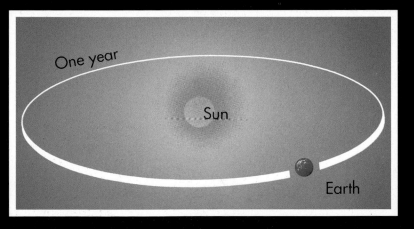

One year

Sun

Earth

than the Earth, and it is a very long way away. The Earth moves around the sun, taking one year to do so. There are eight other bodies of the same kind, which we call planets. Some of the planets have moons; we have one, our own moon, which shines because it is being lit up by the sun. As well as the eight planets and their moons, there are many bodies in the sun's family, including shooting stars and comets.

Sun

Earth

Moon

Earth

The Earth and its air

The Earth is shaped like a ball. We live on its surface, and we do not fly off because of a force called gravity, which holds us all down. If you throw a stone upwards, it will soon fall down again, because the Earth's gravity will not let it go. The air around us is made up of gas. If you swing your hand, you can feel the air being pushed out of the way. But the air does not spread upwards forever. The higher you go, the less air there will be. On the tops of some mountains, the air is so thin that you could not breathe it, and out in space there is no air at all.

Mountaineers need to wear oxygen masks when they are very high up.

6

When you are travelling in space, you seem to have no weight at all.

Shooting stars

If you look into the sky on a dark, clear night, you will see the stars. Stars are suns, and our sun is only a star; it looks brighter than the others only because it is so much closer to us. A streak of light moving quickly across the night sky is

what we call a meteor or shooting star. It is not at all like a real star; it is only a tiny piece of "dust" burning away in the Earth's upper air. Some meteors may become very bright, but they disappear in seconds. They burn away long before they can fall to the ground.

What makes a shooting star?

A meteor moves around the sun in the same way as the Earth does. When it is in space, we cannot see it, because it is much too small. We see it only when it moves into the top of the Earth's air, and becomes hot because of what we call friction.

If you pump up a bicycle tyre, you will find that the pump gets hot, because the air inside it is being squashed; this sets up friction, and this causes heat. A meteor moving into the upper air sets up so much heat by friction against the air that it catches fire, and burns away.

Showers of shooting stars

Meteors usually move around the sun in bunches. When the Earth moves through one of these bunches, it collects a great many pieces of "dust", and the result is a shower of shooting stars.

This happens several times in every year, but the best time to see meteors is in the first part of August, when the Earth passes through a dense bunch. If you look up into a dark, clear sky for a few minutes at any time between the end of July and about August 17, you will probably be lucky enough to see several shooting stars. Of course, you can see them at other times; meteors may appear at any moment.

Tail   Ice

Core

Shooting stars and comets

Meteors come from bodies which are called comets. Comets, too, move around the sun, but they are not like the other planets. A comet is a lump of ice, mixed with "dust". As it moves through space, it leaves a trail of "dust" behind. It is this "dust" which we see as shooting stars, as they fall into the Earth's air.

A comet is a long way away, so that it does not move quickly across the sky in the same way as a meteor. You would have to watch a comet for many hours before you can see that it is moving at all.

Shooting stars are left behind by comets.

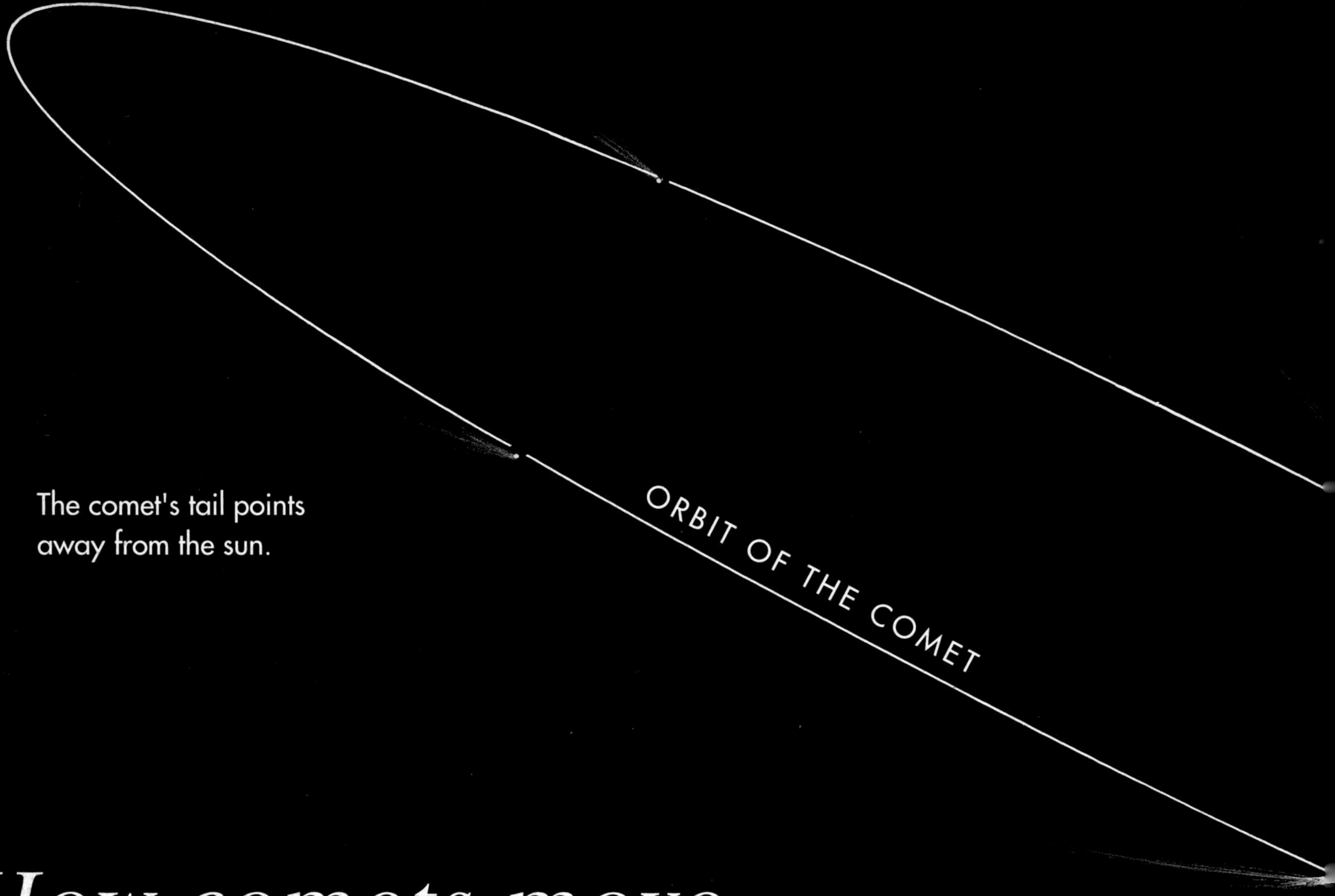

The comet's tail points
away from the sun.

ORBIT OF THE COMET

How comets move The Earth

Earth

goes around the sun in a path which is very like a

circle. A comet has a different sort of path. As you can see from the

picture, a comet may sometimes be much closer to the sun than we

are, while at other times it will be much further away. Some comets

take only a few years to go once around the sun, but others take a very long time indeed – many hundreds or even thousands of years.

A comet shines only because it is being lit up by the sun, so it is

bright only when it is close to us. When it is a long way away, it

becomes so faint that we cannot see it at all.

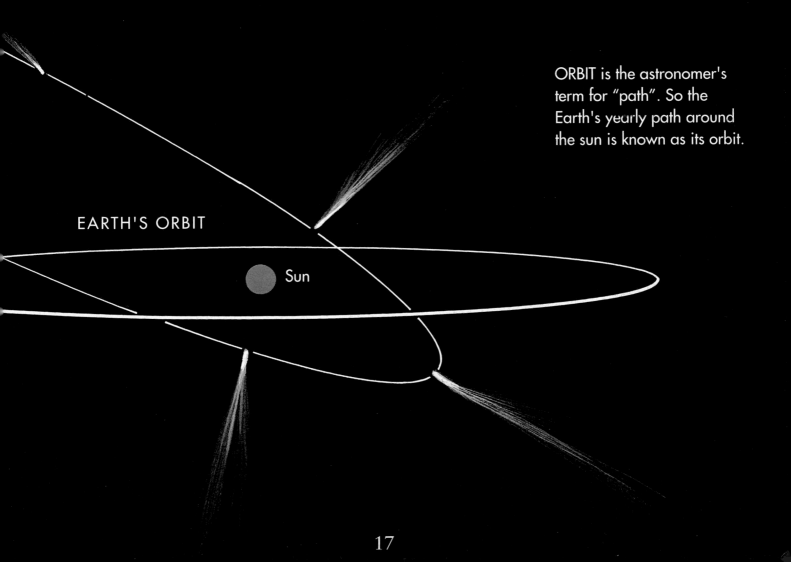

ORBIT is the astronomer's term for "path". So the Earth's yearly path around the sun is known as its orbit.

EARTH'S ORBIT

Sun

The tails of comets

When a comet is a long way from the sun it is very cold, and is nothing more than a frozen lump. When it moves closer to the sun, and is warmed, the icy lump is surrounded by gas, making up what we call the comet's head.

A really big comet may also grow a long tail, stretching away from the sun. There have even been comets which have become so bright that they have cast shadows. No comets like this have been seen for many years now. Most comets are much fainter, and many of them never grow tails at all.

Halley's Comet

The best-known comet is called Halley's Comet, because it was an astronomer named Edmond Halley who first found out that it moves around the sun. It comes back about every 75 years, and has been seen very often; it was in the sky just before the Battle of Hastings, in 1066, when William the Conqueror landed in England!

The Bayeux Tapestry, showing Halley's Comet, is 900 years old.

When it last came back, in 1986, five spaceships were sent to it, and one of these went right through the comet's head, sending back pictures of the icy lump in the middle.

Halley's Comet has now moved away from the sun, and is too faint to be seen, but we know where it is. When it next comes back, in the year 2061, you may be lucky enough to see it for yourself.

Halley's Comet passing the space probe Giotto

Stones from space

Sometimes the Earth meets a body which is big enough to drop right through the air without being burned away. It then lands on the Earth, and is called a meteorite.

Museums keep collections of meteorites; you can see them there. Most are made up of stone and iron. They do not come from comets, and are quite different from shooting star meteors.

A large meteorite may make a large hole or crater; one of these craters, in Arizona, is nearly a mile wide. If a populated area of the Earth were hit by a body of this kind there would be a great deal of damage, but luckily  it is not likely to happen; the crater is very old indeed. Nobody has ever been killed by a stone falling from space, so you can feel quite safe when you go outdoors at night to look for shooting stars!

Index